Perfection in Video Product Design

Terms and Conditions

Table Of Contents

Foreword

Video products are another way of creating product awareness and promoting one's business through the product. The video production is meant to showcase moving images to be done on electronic media. Similar to film making it only defer in the images being recoded electronically rather than on film stock. Get all the info you need here.

Video Product Perfection
Insider Tips On Launching Profit Getting Video Products

Chapter 1:

Synopsis

Using this innovative tool there is a platform available to creating content, video editing and delivering a finished video product for various mediums of exposure.

For the online marketer who cost concerns are high on the priority list, this form of creating material to promote the intended item can be quite a welcomed respite. In almost all cases the video product can be competitively cost effective and definitely cheaper that other tools for promotional use.

The Basics

There are several mediums that can be used to promote an organization, a product or a service and video production is just one of them. Creating the awareness for the product is the primary reason this tool is chosen.

Being an accessible feature that can be used from television advertisements to internet commercials and viral videos this tool is innovative enough in its makeup to cater to all mediums of sourcing the relevant information.

Mainly designed for internet home based businesses it is a tool where interaction with the audience through visual presentations is its key feature.

Broken into two significantly different types of video production are the transactional and the reference style. The transactional video production style is mostly meant to promote a product with the intention of making a sale. For the reference based video product the idea is to get the viewer to navigate further into the website to view more information.

Videos are also great search engine avenues thus using these tools would ensure the site is prominently feature when connective or similar subjects are keyed into the system.

Chapter 2:

Choosing Your Target Market And Subject

Synopsis

Using the video production style the individual can effectively promote the business endeavor planned. This method though comparatively new to the online internet market it is fast proving its worth in terms of being extremely beneficial in creating the awareness of the product towards its target audience.

Your Market

One of the biggest and most effective advantage of the video production is that it allows the content to be visually presented therefore making a clearer impact on the target audience when compared to other tools available for online marketing.

The subject matter is also very important as this should be something that the target audience would be interested in being a part of.

Visual explanations accompanied by visual effect is always more impactful in delivering any message designed especially if it is for marketing purposes.

Being able to get the video product to the end target audience can ideally be done with proper assistance from established companies handling such business promotion styles.

These entities usually are very apt in being able to get the video product to the distributorships that will help further the exposure for the product.

If the video product is suitable as an exhibition tool for the business entity then the companies promoting them will target businesses that priorities such promotional styles.

Video product have been able to successfully pitch revenue earning prospects for various type of business styles and it usually gets the desired attention faster than other more conventional tool can.

Tapping into the target audience segment that spends most of their time in the comforts of their home, through the various different media platforms available, is also another way to get the video products content to the masses.

When it comes to subject matter there would be a very wide choice base to choose from as the possible target audience varies greatly.

Chapter 3:
Visualize Your Complete Product, Write Your Script And Obtain Graphics

Synopsis

Every business venture has to start with a basic idea and video products are no different. Before a video product is launched there are a lot of connecting issues that should be addressed to ensure the prime target audience is reached and the material used to reach them is suitable and effectively designed.

Visualize

In order to successfully design and create the contents of a video product, the individual has to first have an idea of the end results expected.

With this firmly in mind it would be easier to source for and apply the right tools to start making the video product itself. When the video outline has been decided the next step would be to start writing the script for the video content.

Script writing can be done by almost anyone even a novice but if the individual is serious about getting the best possible exposure for the product perhaps considering more professional expertise maybe more beneficial.

Those with the expertise will be able to better design script content that would directly impact the viewer and this should be the ideal impact sought.

Depending on the type of product, business or service being featured in the video product, the script designed should be able to reflect the idea behind the product clearly and effectively. The style of the design would have to suit the content and message intended for the viewing prospects.

Making use of graphics to enhance the content style of the video product is another way of creating as exciting product. Whenever there is extensive use of graphics the end product is usually more exciting and visually attractive.

This is why most well designed video product makes it a point to include good graphics into their designs. Besides being attention grabbing it is also a great interactive style tool that gets the senses of the viewer alerted to the intended message.

Chapter 4:

Choose And Learn Your Editing Software

Synopsis

There are several reasons why there is a need to understand the various aspects of choosing and learning about editing software. Choosing the best editing software to assist in editing exercises will ensure the end video content will be fit for viewing and promotional purposes.

The Tools

Elements like ensuring the editing software chosen should be able to convert the imported video material into other formats that are available to the particular target audience for portable devices that are used to read the video material.

Being able to edit material such as cutting and merging parts of the original material to custom fit the requirements should be explored for its merits.

Not all viewers would need the same content thus the need to edit to custom fit the needs of the niche target audience. There are also editing software that allow for the export and import of video files that can be directly linked to the computer for easy access.

This then becomes a good advantage as there is no further need for any other kinds of plug-ins and downloads. Being able to add in extra effects can also be facilitated with editing software that provides for this feature.

Improving the quality of the video can also be done with the use of good and compatible editing software.

Choosing editing software that allow for size adjustments and graphics to create material that is suitable for smaller screens such as mobile phones should also be seriously explored.

This is mainly due to the fact that mobile phones are a fast and effective tool for advertising anything and everything instantaneously.

Remembering to watermark anywhere to ensure protection for the video copy write ownership is important.

Understanding all these important points will certainly help the individual to keep an informed grasp on every aspect of the video product's creation.

Chapter 5:
Record Audio

Synopsis

The process of learning how to record audio is really not very difficult. However one must be equip with the right tool and some knowledge of how it's done. The items that would be needed are a good quality microphone or input device, a computer with a sound card and an audio recording software. With these tools, one should be able to commence the audio recording session.

The Audio

One of the more popular software used by most people trying to design their own audio presentation is the Record ForAll screen. This is mainly divided into three main sections.

First one will be given access to the library tool where all storage and organizing of the audio clips are done. Here the individual can import songs, sound effects or other audio files by simply clicking on the plus button.

The red button facilitates the recording directly from the microphone or from another live audio feed. All this can then be added to the library already created. The clips can be sorted by title, artist or any other chosen criteria which can then be accessed by clicking on the column headings.

Then the next area to deal with is called the play list and here is where the list of clips is in the current show state. Adding this material to the playlist can be done by dragging the intended item in from the library.

This method can also be used to change the order of items on the playlist. To view the presentation content there is a timeline at the bottom of the screen which shows the same clips but in much more detail.

Each line on the timeline shows a visual representation of how the clip sounds and any part can be accessed by pressing the play button.

When the overall content and presentation has reached the satisfactory level then the show sounds can be sent out with the export button at the top of the screen to export in MP3, WAV or WMA format.

Chapter 6:

Synopsis

Assembling a video for enhancement of the business awareness exercise is another effective way of getting the product to the attention of the target audience intended. This can be done with a few simple ideas that should be incorporated into the video presentation design.

The Visuals

First a decision should be made on what kind of video presentation is to be created. Details such as the type of target audience it is targeted for. Such information will rank in more relevant searches and provide relevant information fields on the page posted.

The tools needed would include digital photos and music, video slideshow software such as DVD slideshow builder for windows or Fantashow for Mac and YouTube or Facebook accounts where registration is free. The following are some step to help in the process of making a video slide show:

Adding photos and music - Download and install DVD slide show builder deluxe software and when this has been launcher enter advance mode and start from organize tab. Then import favorite photos, videos, music to the story board and any other displays to be included in the presentation. If there is any need for it, click media sources for edit purposes.

Changing photo transitions – after importing the photo and video material, random transitions will automatically be applied. However changes can be made to the photo transition by clicking the transition thumb on the story board and selecting the desired transition for the eventual dialog phase. An auto system can also be accessed if the individual does not fancy setting the transitions personally.

Save video to MP4 – go to the create tab and in the output formats drop down list, select MP4 as the prevailing video format. Upon accessing this click start and this will save the video for the chosen platform. If there is a need to customize the video the options button can be clicked thus giving the individual other options.

Chapter 7:

Synopsis

After designing and working on the video the end result that is ready for viewing should now be made available to the target audience as efficiently and as quickly as possible. There are various ways to achieve this and one of them is by going viral.

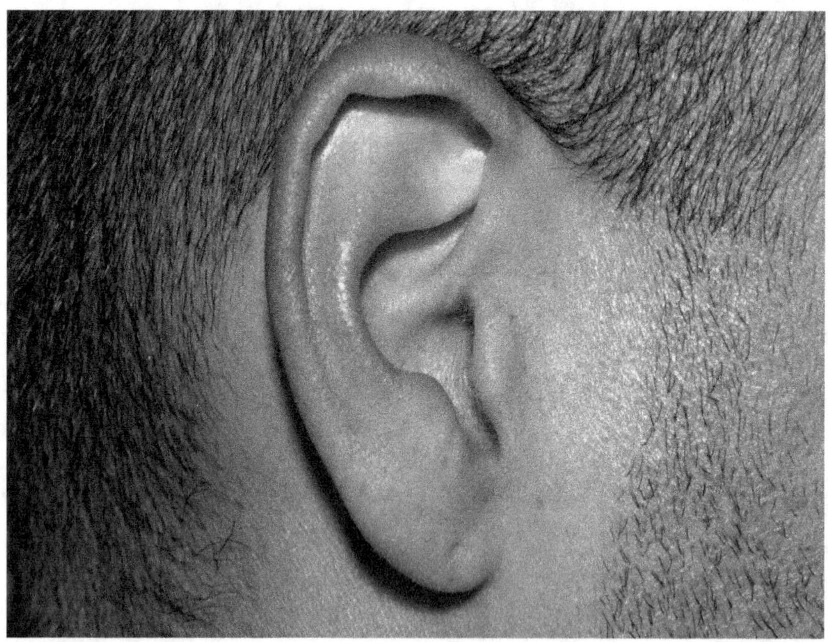

The Buzz

If the intention is to use affiliates and other supporting help to get the video to a target audience that cannot be reached by the individual's own efforts then supplying a sample to each of these potential assisting avenues needs to be done.

When this has been done, then the receiving parties can use other supporting tools individually to make the video viral. Sometimes by using this system there is a higher percentage of making the video go viral as there is more than one source putting the video out for the masses to view it. The more exposure gained the more chances of it going viral.

Creating videos that automatically seed themselves within certain platforms of communities and fan bases will also facilitate the viral factor and ensure its success.

The recipient of such video who are fascinated or attracted to the content will automatically be inclined to share the said content with others thus again creating the viral circumstances.

Designing and posting videos that are unique yet attention grabbing will also get anyone and everyone excited and wanting to view the material for themselves.

It will also ensure more people will share the said video with others. The basic idea behind going viral is that the video becomes a property so hot that everyone wants to be privy to its content at all cost.

Therefore one should always keep in mind this fact when designing the content. Some may think this would mean that there is a need for being bizarre in the style or content but it really means the video needs to stand out if the massive attention is to be engaged.

Chapter 8:

Launch Your Final Product

Synopsis

Being able to successfully launch a product does not necessarily means having a lot of fanfare or a big budget. There are ways to be able to do this especially online with comparatively minimal cost and definite just as effectively. Therefore it is possible to launch a product with a small budget and the knowledge of tools that could assist and enhance the exercise.

Getting It Going

Understanding that the purpose of the launch is to build the momentum of the sales positioning and eventual revenue earned is important.

Thus working within this understanding should ideally yield the desired results. The following are tips to consider while working within the above mentioned mindset:

The important point of matching product capabilities to the market needs is perhaps one that should be given due consideration.

Identifying the ideal market positioning will create the advantage of being able to tap into the target audience with a higher percentage of success. Ensure the launch is designed around a clear positioning and messaging platform.

Setting clear launch goals will help the individual or team work with tangible tactics on how to tackle and constantly evaluate the progress. At this point ensuring all the complimenting tools are also used to optimization would help enhance the launch.

Wrapping Up

Creating the perception of adequate leverage and capitalizing on it is another way to ensure optimal launch results. The leverage used should ideally be based on the concept of using little to gain much, which is possible through the use of some internet marketing tools.

Getting help from all sources available, especially from within the extended circle working on the launch would effectively contribute to the agenda being conveniently publicized. Publicity especially when it is of the positive nature is always a great crowd puller.

Setting the pace for the interest for the product featured in the video would generally yield good results.

www.ingramcontent.com/pod-product-compliance
Lightning Source LLC
LaVergne TN
LVHW050309200726
843509LV00015B/3234